PUBLIC LIBRARY

INSIDE MLB

CINCINNATI
REDS

BY ANTHONY K. HEWSON

SportsZone

An Imprint of Abdo Publishing
abdobooks.com

abdobooks.com

Published by Abdo Publishing, a division of ABDO, PO Box 398166, Minneapolis, Minnesota 55439. Copyright © 2023 by Abdo Consulting Group, Inc. International copyrights reserved in all countries. No part of this book may be reproduced in any form without written permission from the publisher. SportsZone™ is a trademark and logo of Abdo Publishing.

Printed in the United States of America, North Mankato, Minnesota.
102022
012023

THIS BOOK CONTAINS RECYCLED MATERIALS

Cover Photo: Joe Robbins/Icon Sportswire/AP Images
Interior Photos: Jamie Sabau/Getty Images Sport/Getty Images, 4; Mark Rucker/Transcendental Graphics/Getty Images Sport/Getty Images, 8; Charles Conlan/Transcendental Graphics/Getty Images, 10; FPG/Hulton Archive/Getty Images, 11; George Rinhart/Corbis Historical/Getty Images, 12; AP Images, 15, 17, 21; Bettmann/Getty Images, 18, 22; Focus on Sport/Getty Images, 24, 26, 28, 29, 31, 32; Mark Lyons/AP Images, 34; David Durochik/AP Images, 35; Tom DiPace/AP Images, 37; Al Behrman/AP Images, 40; Paul Ward/MLB/Getty Images, 41

Editor: Charlie Beattie
Series Designer: Becky Daum

Library of Congress Control Number: 2022940397

Publisher's Cataloging-in-Publication Data
Names: Hewson, Anthony K., author.
Title: Cincinnati Reds / by Anthony K. Hewson
Description: Minneapolis, Minnesota: Abdo Publishing, 2023 | Series: Inside MLB | Includes online resources and index.
Identifiers: ISBN 9781098290146 (lib. bdg.) | ISBN 9781098275341 (ebook)
Subjects: LCSH: Cincinnati Reds (Baseball team)--Juvenile literature. | Baseball teams--Juvenile literature. | Professional sports--Juvenile literature. | Sports franchises--Juvenile literature. | Major League Baseball (Organization)--Juvenile literature.
Classification: DDC 796.35764--dc23

TABLE OF CONTENTS

CHAPTER 1
THE RED STOCKINGS 4

CHAPTER 2
TURN ON THE LIGHTS 12

CHAPTER 3
THE BIG RED MACHINE 22

CHAPTER 4
ROLLING DOWN THE RIVER .. 32

TIMELINE 42
TEAM FACTS 44
TEAM TRIVIA 45
GLOSSARY 46
MORE INFORMATION 47
ONLINE RESOURCES 47
INDEX 48
ABOUT THE AUTHOR 48

CHAPTER 1

THE RED STOCKINGS

The 2020 baseball season had just three days remaining. Opportunities for the Cincinnati Reds to clinch a playoff spot were running out. And Cincinnati's game that night was down to its final outs. Mike Moustakas stepped into the batter's box in the ninth inning with a chance to make a difference.

Moustakas was new to the Reds in 2020. Veterans like him were key to Cincinnati's playoff hopes. The second baseman had plenty of experience and was a World Series champion with the 2015 Kansas City Royals. Moustakas was also having a great game. In the fourth inning, he hammered a slider from Minnesota Twins starter Jose Berrios out to center field.

Mike Moustakas's heroics helped the Reds secure a playoff spot in 2020.

That solo home run put the Reds up 2–1. The Reds took a 4–2 lead into the ninth.

Moustakas now looked to put the game out of reach. Twins reliever Edwar Colina started the at-bat with a ball. He then offered a slider down and in. Moustakas was ready. He turned on the pitch and sent it high down the right-field line. The ball kept flying in the cool fall night and landed in the seats. It was 5–2 Reds.

By the end of the inning, Cincinnati was up 7–2. Then Wade Miley shut down the Twins in the bottom of the ninth. The left-hander fielded the final ground ball himself. As he flipped it to first baseman Joey Votto to end the game, the rest of the Reds jumped out of the dugout to celebrate. One of baseball's oldest teams was headed back to the playoffs.

OHIO ORIGINALS

The Reds' long history began with a much longer nickname. The Cincinnati Red Stockings were original members of the National League (NL) in 1876. But those were not the same Reds of today. That Cincinnati team was kicked out of the NL in 1880 for rules violations such as scheduling games on Sundays. That day was reserved for worship and rest.

The current version of the team was born in 1881. After one year as an independent team, the Red Stockings joined the rival American Association (AA) in 1882. Cincinnati won the league title in its first year. That was the only AA championship for the Red Stockings. But they scored an even bigger victory when they were allowed back into the NL for the 1890 season. It was then that they shortened their name simply to Reds.

In Cincinnati's early days, Opening Day became a special tradition. The Reds were the southernmost NL team. Their warmer weather meant the Reds were nearly always picked to be home on Opening Day. Soon the return of baseball each spring turned into an official holiday in Cincinnati.

THE FIRST PROS

The first version of the Cincinnati Red Stockings was founded in 1866. In 1869 the Red Stockings began paying players and became the first fully professional team in baseball. Paying players had previously been banned. With money to offer, the Red Stockings could attract the best players in the world. That year, Cincinnati finished 57–0.

BUILDING A WINNER

The Reds had a permanent name and a permanent league. They also had one of the most unique ballparks of the era. At the time, most stadiums were built out of wood. In 1902 the Reds opened a ballpark made from iron and concrete, much like modern parks today. The grand park had an equally grand name—the Palace of the Fans.

The Palace of the Fans was the envy of other MLB teams when it was built in 1902.

The fans that packed into the Palace didn't see any championships, however. The Reds finished no higher than fourth in the 10 years the Palace was open. After a fire nearly destroyed the stadium in 1911, the Reds built a new park on the same spot. Redland Field opened the next season. It would be the home of Cincinnati's baseball team for the next 60 years.

Redland Field didn't see a lot of winning in its early years, either. But things started to turn around in 1918. Cincinnati climbed to third in the NL. In 1919 the Reds were truly ready to compete. They won a team-record 96 games and easily captured their first NL title.

Cincinnati's lineup was powerful. Center fielder Edd Roush won the batting title and led the Reds with 71 runs batted in (RBIs). Third baseman Heinie Groh was right behind him with 63. Pitchers Slim Sallee, Dutch Ruether, and Hod Eller combined to win 59 games.

THE 1919 WORLD SERIES

Cincinnati had a better record than the 1919 American League (AL) champion Chicago White Sox. But the upstart Reds were still considered an underdog in the World Series. Many were surprised when Cincinnati knocked around Chicago ace Eddie Cicotte in a 9–1 Game 1 victory.

OFFICIALLY RED

The Reds officially began using that name in 1890. But they didn't wear it on their uniforms until 1913. That was the year the team added the word "REDS" to the inside of the C logo they had been wearing for years. The team still wears a version of that logo today.

The Reds then beat another tough Sox starter, Lefty Williams, in Game 2. Chicago rebounded to win Game 3, but Cincinnati won the next two and didn't allow a run. In the best-of-nine-game series, the Reds were one win away from their first championship.

With the series back in Cincinnati, the Sox suddenly found new life. They won Game 6 and Game 7, with Cicotte getting the Game 7 win. But the Reds still had two more chances to win the series.

Outfielder Edd Roush won two batting titles in 12 years with the Reds after joining the team in 1916.

Despite his struggles in the series, Williams got the start for Chicago. The Reds jumped on him early. And Eller was solid as the Reds raced to a 10–5 win.

Reds players hold up a banner celebrating their 1919 World Series title.

Not long after the Reds celebrated their first World Series victory, the games began to make news of a very different kind. The baseball world would soon learn that members of the 1919 White Sox had been offered money by gamblers to intentionally lose the World Series. An investigation resulted in eight Sox players being banned from baseball for life. The "Black Sox" scandal overshadowed the Reds' championship.

However, many Reds players and their fans remained proud. For the rest of his life, Roush angrily denied that the Reds did not fully deserve their title. But the 1919 World Series is still remembered more for what the White Sox were accused of than what the Reds accomplished.

CHAPTER 2

TURN ON THE LIGHTS

Reds fans looked to the 1920 season with great excitement. Their team was the reigning World Series champion. And while Opening Day had become a yearly celebration in Cincinnati, 1920 brought an even bigger tradition.

Parades were a typical event on Opening Day. In 1920 Cincinnati's Findlay Market organized the biggest parade yet. Every year since, the Findlay Market Opening Day Parade has been held on Opening Day in Cincinnati. In that time, Cincinnati has opened at home every season except 1966 and 1990.

Third baseman Heinie Groh hit .298 over nine seasons with the Reds and led the NL in doubles twice.

The rest of the 1920 season didn't live up to the fanfare. The Reds spent much of the year in first place, but a 3–15 stretch in September saw the team crash out of the race. By the end of the season, they were 10 1/2 games behind the NL champion Brooklyn Robins.

THE CROSLEY TERRACE

One of the most famous features of Crosley Field was the terrace in left field. Starting 20 feet (6.1 m) from the outfield wall, the field began to slope upward. Climbing the terrace to catch a fly ball was a unique challenge for visiting outfielders. The terrace was the last outfield hill in MLB until the Houston Astros opened what is now Minute Maid Park in 2000.

BIG CHANGES

As the 1920s wore on, the Reds struggled to compete both on and off the field. By 1933 team owner Sidney Weil could no longer pay the Reds' bills. A bank took away possession of the team.

Many Reds fans were worried that the next owner would move the team out of town. Powel Crosley Jr. was one such fan. But Crosley had enough money to do something about it. He had made a fortune in the auto and radio industries. Reds games already aired on a radio station Crosley owned. In 1934 he stepped up and bought the team. Even though the Reds finished 52–99 that season, it was a huge year for Cincinnati.

The Reds defeated the Philadelphia Phillies 2–1 in the first night game in MLB history.

Crosley made big changes to Redland Field, starting with the name. The Reds' home was renamed Crosley Field. The Reds also became the first team in the majors to use an airplane for a road trip.

The next season, the Reds changed the look of baseball forever. On May 24, the first night game in Major League Baseball (MLB) history took place at Crosley Field. President Franklin D. Roosevelt pushed the button to turn on the newly installed lights. Installing the lights cost $50,000—which is more than $1,000,000 in today's money.

Night games helped double the team's attendance from 1934 to 1935. And the Reds won 16 more games. They climbed out of last place for the first time in four years.

NO-NO'S

Crosley's investments made the Reds winners again by 1938. They finished fourth in the NL, but it was a summer to remember for fans. The biggest reason was pitcher Johnny Vander Meer. On June 11, the lefty made the 10th start of his first full season in the big leagues. He showed the dominance he was capable of. Vander Meer didn't allow a single hit in a 3–0 win over the Boston Bees. He didn't even allow a runner to get to second base.

Vander Meer wasn't quite as sharp in his next start. On June 15 he walked eight Brooklyn Dodgers. He even walked the bases full in the ninth. But Vander Meer stepped up when he had to. He retired Brooklyn shortstop Leo Durocher on a fly ball to end the game. Vander Meer had another no-hitter.

No pitcher had ever thrown back-to-back no-hitters. Vander Meer went on to make four All-Star Games and was a fixture in the Reds' pitching rotation for 13 seasons. But his finest moments came over four days in June 1938.

THREE MVPs

Vander Meer was one of four Reds starting the 1938 All-Star Game at Crosley Field. Ernie Lombardi was the starting catcher. Lombardi was also behind the plate for both of Vander Meer's no-hitters.

Johnny Vander Meer made four All-Star teams while playing for the Reds and led the NL in strikeouts three times.

    Lombardi had an even bigger impact as a hitter, winning two batting titles. His 1938 title also came with NL Most Valuable Player (MVP) honors, a first in Reds history.

    The next season the Reds were ready to challenge for the NL title. Vander Meer was an All-Star, as was 32-year-old righty Paul Derringer. But the Reds' ace was Bucky Walters. A former third baseman who converted to pitching, Walters won an NL-best 27 games. The right-hander also led the NL in

Pitchers Paul Derringer, *left,* **and Bucky Walters,** *right,* **as well as catcher Ernie Lombardi,** *center,* **were three of Cincinnati's key players during the team's World Series runs of 1939 and 1940.**

earned-run average (ERA) and strikeouts. At the end of the year, he was the team's second straight NL MVP.

At 97–57 the Reds won the NL by 4 1/2 games. With no playoffs at the time, Cincinnati was back in the World Series for the first time since 1919. Waiting for the Reds were the three-time defending champions, the New York Yankees. Derringer lost the first game 2–1. New York then beat Walters 4–0 in Game 2. The offense picked up back in Cincinnati, but New York took each of the next two games to claim its fourth championship in a row.

In 1940 the Reds were even better, at 100–53. Walters and Derringer both finished in the top five in MVP voting. They lost out to yet another Reds teammate. First baseman Frank McCormick hit .309 with 19 home runs and 127 RBIs to take the award.

This time the Reds faced the Detroit Tigers in the World Series. After Detroit took a 3–2 lead, Walters pitched a five-hit shutout in Game 6. Derringer took the hill in Game 7 and quickly fell behind 1–0. But the Reds rallied in the seventh inning. Back-to-back doubles by McCormick and left fielder Jimmy Ripple tied the game. Ripple then scored on a sacrifice fly from shortstop Billy Meyers. Derringer took over from there. With the game still 2–1, he got three ground-outs in the top of the ninth inning. This time there was no controversy. The Reds were World Series champions.

BACK INTO DECLINE

The Reds were unable to maintain their World Series form as older players like Derringer and Walters became less effective. Cincinnati spent most of the next 20 years in the bottom half of the NL standings. Hosting the 1953 All-Star Game helped the Reds show off stars like slugger Ted Kluszewski. He went on to lead the NL in homers in 1954.

The Reds made bigger news off the field. In the early 1950s, the United States was very concerned with the threat of a form of government called communism, which was used in the Soviet Union. The fear was given the name "Red Scare" after the color of the Soviet flag. Not wanting to be caught up in the politics of the time, the Cincinnati Reds decided to change their name. Just before the 1953 season, the Reds became the Redlegs. They used the name until 1958 before quietly changing it back.

Cincinnati slugger Ted Kluszewski famously cut the sleeves off his uniform. He said doing so freed up his arms to swing harder.

CHAPTER 3

THE BIG RED MACHINE

In 1956 a quiet, fiercely competitive outfielder named Frank Robinson made his debut for Cincinnati. He hit 38 home runs, made the All-Star team, and won NL Rookie of the Year. Meanwhile, the Reds won 91 games, their best finish since the championship season of 1940.

It wasn't good enough to make the World Series, but Robinson's arrival was the start of a turnaround that would last for more than two decades. More big moves followed. In 1961 the Reds brought in Bill DeWitt as general manager. The team had finished sixth a year earlier and was hoping to bounce back. It didn't take long. Led by Robinson's MVP season, Cincinnati reached the World Series in DeWitt's first year.

Frank Robinson topped 30 home runs seven times in 10 years with the Reds.

Pete Rose hit over .300 every year from 1965 to 1973 and won the NL batting title three times during that stretch.

Once again, the mighty New York Yankees shut down the Reds for a 4–1 series victory. But DeWitt was just getting started. After the series was over, he made his biggest move yet. DeWitt bought the Reds from the Crosley family.

In total control of the team, DeWitt brought in more young stars. The 1963 season saw the debut of 22-year-old second baseman Pete Rose. The switch hitter would eventually earn the nickname "Charlie Hustle" for his relentless style of play. Rose was named 1963 NL Rookie of the Year.

Chasing another NL title in 1964, the Reds surged into first place with just a few games left. They were tied with the St. Louis Cardinals with one game left to play. However, while the Cardinals won against the Mets in St. Louis, the Reds lost at home to the Philadelphia Phillies, ending their season.

That was the best the Reds could do in the 1960s. The Cardinals and Los Angeles Dodgers dominated the NL. And in 1965 DeWitt made a huge mistake. Looking for more pitching, he traded Robinson to the Baltimore Orioles for three players. Robinson played another 11 years and won an AL MVP in 1966. None of the players the Reds received turned into stars.

Despite what is considered one of the worst trades in MLB history, DeWitt left the Reds in good shape when he sold the team in 1966. They still had Rose, along with young third baseman Tony Pérez. And more stars were on the way.

STARTING THE MACHINE

By 1970 the Reds were loaded. Young players signed or drafted by DeWitt littered the lineup. Johnny Bench was just 22 years old but already considered the best catcher in baseball, both offensively and defensively. He hit 45 home runs, while Pérez added 40. Rose, now an outfielder, had more than 200 hits

Catcher Johnny Bench won Rookie of the Year and two MVP Awards in his first five full MLB seasons.

for the third straight season. Another skilled 22-year-old, shortstop Dave Concepción, made his debut.

Leading the team was a new manager. George "Sparky" Anderson had been an MLB player for just one year, in 1959. He wasn't very good. But he was a brilliant leader. When he took over the Reds in 1970, he had never been an MLB manager. It didn't matter. Anderson led the Reds to a 102–60 record. Cincinnati then swept the Pittsburgh Pirates in the NL Championship Series (NLCS), which had debuted a year earlier. While the Reds lost the World Series to Robinson's Orioles, Cincinnati was just getting started.

In 1969 a Cincinnati sportswriter coined the nickname "the Big Red Machine" for the Reds. As the team plowed through the NL in the 1970s, the name took off. Though the Reds struggled in 1971, they bounced back with a big season the next year. Now playing in a new home, Riverfront Stadium, the Reds added more stars. Second baseman Joe Morgan came over in a trade. So did power-hitting outfielder George Foster. A 95-win season was followed by another World Series appearance. However, this one ended in heartbreak with a seven-game loss to the Oakland Athletics.

THE GREAT EIGHT

It took three more years for the Big Red Machine to get back to the World Series. The 1975 team was one of the best baseball has ever seen. The steady-hitting Morgan was named NL MVP. Rose led the league in runs scored and doubles. Bench and Pérez each drove in more than 100 runs. Concepción, Foster, center fielder César Gerónimo, and right fielder Ken Griffey rounded out the Reds' "Great Eight." The pitching staff had three 15-game winners in Jack Billingham, Gary Nolan, and Don Gullett. Anderson led the team to its best-ever record of 108–54. Cincinnati then shut down the Pirates in a three-game NLCS sweep.

NEARLY HISTORY

Former all-time home run leader Hank Aaron hit some big homers in Cincinnati. In 1970 he hit the first home run at Riverfront Stadium. On Opening Day in 1974, Aaron hit his 714th homer at Riverfront while playing for the Atlanta Braves to tie Babe Ruth for the most ever. Aaron didn't get a hit in the rest of the series and broke the record at home days later.

The Reds' Great Eight lineup consisted of, *from left*, Pete Rose, Joe Morgan, Johnny Bench, Tony Pérez, George Foster, Dave Concepción, Ken Griffey, and César Gerónimo.

That set up a matchup with the Boston Red Sox in the World Series. Both teams were looking for their first titles in many years. The Reds had not won since 1940. The Red Sox had last won in 1918. The two championship-starved clubs then battled in an epic seven-game series. All but two of the games were decided by a single run. Game 6 is considered one of the greatest World Series games of all time. Playing in Boston, Cincinnati had a 6–3 lead going into the bottom of the eighth. Six more outs would win the World Series for the Reds. But a three-run homer tied the game for Boston. The Red Sox then had a chance to win it in the bottom of the ninth. Foster threw out Boston's Denny Doyle at home plate after Doyle tried to advance on a sacrifice fly. Red Sox catcher Carlton Fisk finally ended the game with a famous home run in the bottom of the 12th inning.

The Reds celebrated their first World Series title in 35 years after beating the Boston Red Sox in 1975.

The series moved to Game 7, and Boston jumped out to a 3–0 lead. A Pérez two-run homer in the sixth started Cincinnati's comeback. The Reds tied it in the seventh, and the game stayed that way into the ninth inning. Morgan came up with two outs and runners on first and third. He popped a single to center off the end of his bat. Griffey trotted home with the go-ahead run. Boston failed to score in the bottom half of the inning. The Big Red Machine had finally brought a championship back to Cincinnati.

Baseball had been struggling for attendance in the 1970s. The exciting 1975 World Series helped bring many fans back. Anderson summed up the seven magical games very simply: "I don't know that there's ever been a better World Series."

BACK-TO-BACK

No NL team had won back-to-back World Series since the New York Giants of 1921 and 1922. In 1976 the Big Red Machine made that challenge look easy. Cincinnati led the NL in nearly every offensive category. Morgan, a future Hall of Famer, won MVP again. The Reds' 102 wins were 10 better than the second-place Los Angeles Dodgers in the NL West Division.

Cincinnati dominated the playoffs. The Philadelphia Phillies had won 101 games during the regular season. But the Reds swept Philadelphia in three games during the NLCS. Next up were the Yankees in the World Series. Cincinnati's pitchers held New York to eight runs in four games. Bench earned MVP honors by hitting 8-for-15 (.533) with two home runs and six RBIs. His second homer was a three-run shot in the ninth inning of Game 4 at Yankee Stadium. It broke open a 7–2 win as the Reds swept.

THE MACHINE BREAKS DOWN

The Big Red Machine never reached those heights again. For the rest of the 1970s, individual highlights kept Cincinnati fans entertained. Foster was MVP in 1977 after hitting a team-record 52 home runs. The next year, Rose put together a 44-game hitting streak. It was the longest in MLB since the Yankees' Joe DiMaggio set the record of 56 straight in 1941.

Joe Morgan drove in a career-high 111 runs in 1976.

Cincinnati reached the playoffs again in 1979 but was swept in the NLCS by the Pirates. By then Pérez and Rose were already gone. When the team suited up for the 1982 season, only Bench and Concepción remained from the Great Eight. That year the Reds finished 61–101. It was time to start over.

CHAPTER 4

ROLLING DOWN THE RIVER

Johnny Bench retired after the 1983 season. His 327 home runs as a catcher were, at the time, a record for the position. His manager, Sparky Anderson, said, "I don't want to embarrass any other catchers by comparing them to Johnny Bench."

Although Cincinnati was losing one legend, others came back. Tony Pérez and Pete Rose returned in 1984 to play their final three seasons in Cincinnati. Rose also served as manager as he chased one of baseball's greatest records.

On September 11, 1985, Rose slapped a single into left-center field for his 4,192nd career hit. That passed

Pete Rose salutes the fans from first base after recording his 4,192nd career hit on September 11, 1985.

Reds players congratulate Tom Browning, *center*, after he pitched a perfect game against the Los Angeles Dodgers on September 16, 1988.

legendary Detroit Tiger Ty Cobb to make Rose baseball's all-time hit king.

The next season was Rose's last as a player. He stayed on as manager and oversaw an exciting young team. The Reds now had athletic outfielder Eric Davis. They also had promising shortstop Barry Larkin, a native of Cincinnati. In 1987 Davis became the first Red to hit 30 homers and steal 30 bases in a season. The summer of 1988 saw the Reds host the All-Star Game. Left-hander Tom Browning also threw the first perfect game in team history.

Things were looking good for the Reds. They had put together four consecutive winning seasons. But in 1989 a scandal rocked the team and all of MLB. Rose was under investigation for gambling on baseball while managing the Reds. Betting on games was strictly prohibited by MLB rules. Rose not only had to leave the Reds but also was banned from baseball for life. Baseball's all-time hit king would never enter the Hall of Fame.

THE NASTY BOYS

To replace Rose, the Reds turned to Lou Piniella. An All-Star as a player in the 1970s, Piniella was known for his fiery competitiveness. In an August 1990 game, he famously removed first base and threw it into right field while arguing a call at Riverfront Stadium.

Piniella had reason to be fired up. His Reds were shocking the baseball world as they jumped up the NL West standings. The surprising Reds never fell out of first place in winning the division.

While Davis and Larkin led the offense, the team's strength was its bullpen. The relief trio of Rob Dibble, Norm Charlton, and Randy Myers was nearly impossible to hit. And their fierce reputation on the mound earned them the nickname "the Nasty Boys." If the Reds had a lead late in games, the Nasty Boys were likely to hold it.

Rob Dibble struck out 136 batters in just 98 innings for the Reds in 1990.

HATCHER'S HEROICS

The unlikely hero of the Reds' World Series win in 1990 was outfielder Billy Hatcher. After hitting .276 during the season, Hatcher collected nine hits in 15 at-bats against Oakland. His seven straight hits in Games 1 and 2 set a World Series record. Despite his amazing efforts, Hatcher did not win series MVP. That honor went to pitcher José Rijo, who allowed only one run in 15 1/3 innings on the mound.

The Reds were still huge underdogs heading into the World Series. They faced a defending-champion Oakland Athletics team that finished 103–59. The Reds were 91–71.

Davis gave the Reds a dream start in the first inning of Game 1. He hit the first pitch he saw for a two-run home run. The Reds went on to win 7–0. They then won a tense Game 2 in 10 innings. Billy Bates, who had just five at-bats in the regular season, singled and scored the winning run to put the Reds up 2–0 in the series.

The Reds went to Oakland and finished off the improbable sweep. Myers earned the save in Game 4 to kick off a huge celebration. The Reds were honored with a parade as the city celebrated one of MLB's most unlikely championships.

CAPTAIN BARRY

While the Reds struggled to match the magic of 1990, the club had a true star in Larkin. Beloved in his hometown, the shortstop could hit for both power and average and had a

Shortstop Barry Larkin won three Gold Gloves and nine Silver Slugger Awards in his 19-year career.

great glove. He was also the team leader, serving as the Reds' captain. But while he made 12 career All-Star appearances, Larkin played in the playoffs only one other time. The Reds made the postseason during his MVP season of 1995. They were swept in the NLCS by the Atlanta Braves.

One of the Reds' main issues was their owner. Marge Schott had bought the team in 1984. Her ownership included a World Series win and some things fans loved such as affordable hot dogs and tickets. However, Schott attracted many controversies. She hated spending money on player salaries. She often didn't listen to the advice of team scouts. Even worse, allegations of racism followed Schott for years. She was suspended from the team for a year in 1993 and sold the Reds in 1999.

A NEW RIVERFRONT HOME

In 1996 Riverfront Stadium was renamed Cinergy Field. Just six years later, the Reds said goodbye to the park where they won three World Series titles. A new era began just a few feet away as Great American Ball Park (GABP) opened right next door. Unlike Riverfront, which also hosted the Bengals of pro football, GABP was built just for baseball. It had all the modern features that fans hoped for.

It was also a great place to hit. Built on a smaller space than Riverfront, the park had to have shorter distances to the outfield walls. As a result, hitters frequently blasted balls over the fences. Over its first 18 seasons, GABP saw more home runs than any other ballpark.

That was great news for the Reds' sluggers. And the Reds had plenty of them. Adam Dunn led the NL in strikeouts each year from 2004 to 2006. But he also clubbed 40 or more homers in each of those seasons.

Center fielder Ken Griffey Jr. joined the Reds in 2000. The son of former "Big Red Machine" star Ken Griffey hit 210 of his 630 career home runs for his hometown team. But Griffey Jr.'s nine years with the Reds were notable also for his many injuries.

While Cincinnati hitters loved GABP, Cincinnati pitchers struggled to get outs. The Reds were last or next to last in the NL in runs allowed in four of the first five seasons in their new home.

CARVING OUT

The site where Great American Ball Park was built was not very big. To make room, the team had to cut out a section of center field at Riverfront Stadium. That opened up views of the Ohio River to fans during the time the new ballpark was being finished.

JOEY MVP

By 2010 the Reds had enough quality pitchers to balance out the team. Starters Bronson Arroyo and Johnny Cueto were reliable arms. And the Reds had the best offense in baseball, led by first baseman Joey Votto.

Votto could hit for both power and average. The Canadian slugger was runner-up in Rookie of the Year voting in 2008. In 2010 the left-handed hitter was an All-Star for the first time. He also won MVP that year with a .324 average and 37 homers.

Joey Votto rounds the bases after hitting a home run in 2010.

Behind Votto and slick-fielding second baseman Brandon Phillips, the 2010 Reds won the NL Central for the first time in 15 years. But their powerful bats went quiet in the playoffs, and they were swept by the Philadelphia Phillies.

Cincinnati won the division again in 2012. An NLDS loss to the San Francisco Giants sent the Reds home early again. Cincinnati didn't make it past the wild card game in 2013. Many of the same problems affected the Reds throughout the 2010s. They had some strong hitters, but not enough pitching to contend for a championship.

BACK FOR MORE

The Reds solved their pitching problem in a big way in 2020. Since the Cy Young Award was introduced to reward the season's top pitcher in 1956, no Red had ever won it. Righty Trevor Bauer became the first in a season shortened to 60 games by the COVID-19 pandemic.

That helped the Reds get back to the playoffs, but a weak offense doomed Cincinnati. The Reds hit just .212 as a team in 2020, even with the addition of several veterans around Votto. Atlanta shut out the Reds twice for a sweep in the best-of-three NL wild-card series.

The Reds lost Bauer as a free agent after the season. And after missing the playoffs in 2021,

Hunter Greene's fastball has been clocked as high as 103 miles per hour (165.8 km/h).

several more stars left as well. Votto remained, surrounded by young players like 2021 NL Rookie of the Year second baseman Jonathan India.

As 2022 opened, Reds fans got a look at what they hoped was the team's future. Former top draft pick Hunter Greene made his debut. The 22-year-old pitcher routinely throws more than 100 miles per hour (160.9 km/h). Cincinnati fans hope Greene is the first of a new group of Reds heroes.

TIMELINE

1876
The Cincinnati Red Stockings join the National League for its inaugural season.

1882
After getting kicked out of the NL and reforming, the Red Stockings join the American Association and win the league title during their first season.

1890
Cincinnati rejoins the NL for good and shortens its nickname to Reds.

1919
The Reds win the NL title for the first time and face the Chicago White Sox in the World Series, defeating them in eight games. The victory is overshadowed by a gambling scandal involving the White Sox.

1935
The Reds play in the first night game in MLB history at their home ballpark, Crosley Field.

1940
Frank McCormick becomes the third consecutive Red to win MVP honors, and Cincinnati beats the Detroit Tigers to win its second World Series.

1956
Outfielder Frank Robinson makes his MLB debut and wins Rookie of the Year.

1959
After changing their name to Redlegs for six seasons, Cincinnati makes a final name change back to Reds.

1975
Led by MVP Joe Morgan, the "Big Red Machine" core of players win their first World Series together in a thrilling seven-game victory over the Boston Red Sox.

1976
Morgan repeats as MVP and the Reds repeat as champions, sweeping the New York Yankees.

1985
Player/manager Pete Rose collects his 4,192nd hit on May 11, passing Ty Cobb as baseball's all-time leader.

1989
Due to a gambling scandal, Rose is banned from the major leagues for life.

1990
The "Nasty Boys" bullpen comes up big as the Reds make a surprising run to a World Series championship.

2003
The Reds open Great American Ball Park right next door to their former home, Cinergy Field.

2010
Slugger Joey Votto becomes the first Reds player to win MVP since Barry Larkin in 1995.

2020
Trevor Bauer wins the first Cy Young Award in Reds history as Cincinnati returns to the playoffs.

TEAM FACTS

FRANCHISE HISTORY
Cincinnati Red Stockings (1881–1889)
Cincinnati Reds (1890–1953, 1959–)
Cincinnati Redlegs (1954–58)

WORLD SERIES CHAMPIONSHIPS
1919, 1940, 1975, 1976, 1990

KEY PLAYERS
Johnny Bench (1967–83)
Dave Concepción (1970–88)
Paul Derringer (1933–42)
George Foster (1971–81)
Heinie Groh (1913–21)
Barry Larkin (1986–2004)
Ernie Lombardi (1932–41)
Frank McCormick (1934, 1937–46)
Joe Morgan (1972–79)
Tony Pérez (1964–76, 1984–86)
José Rijo (1988–95, 2001–02)
Frank Robinson (1956–65)
Pete Rose (1963–78, 1984–86)
Edd Roush (1916–26)
Johnny Vander Meer (1937–43, 1946–49)
Joey Votto (2007–)
Bucky Walters (1938–48)

KEY MANAGERS
Sparky Anderson (1970–78)
Bill McKechnie (1938–46)
Lou Piniella (1990–92)

HOME STADIUMS
Bank Street Grounds (1882–83)
League Park I (1884–93)
League Park II (1894–1901)
Palace of the Fans (1902–11)
Crosley Field (1912–70)
   Also known as:
   Redland Field (1912–33)
Cinergy Field (1970–2002)
   Also known as:
   Riverfront Stadium (1970–96)
Great American Ball Park (2003–)

TEAM TRIVIA

PUNCHLESS IN THE PLAYOFFS

The 2010 playoffs started off as poorly as possible for the Reds. They became just the second team ever to record zero hits in a postseason game. Roy Halladay of the Philadelphia Phillies struck out eight Reds and walked only one.

YOUNG JOE

World War II (1939–45) put a strain on baseball teams as players left to serve their country. In need of replacements, the Reds turned to 15-year-old Joe Nuxhall in 1944. Nuxhall was the youngest player to appear in an MLB game. It took him eight years to make his next appearance, and he then went on to an All-Star career.

YOU'RE A FIREWORK

The first night game in MLB history also featured the first fireworks display in MLB history. The Ohio company that put on the display still does shows at Reds games today.

WHAT DO YOU C?

The Reds' *C* logo may look familiar. Known as a "wishbone" shape because of the point in the middle, this type of *C* is also worn by the Chicago Bears of pro football and several colleges. Most think the logo was first used by the University of Chicago in 1898, but the Reds were the first professional team to use it, in 1905.

GLOSSARY

ace
A team's best starting pitcher.

bullpen
The area on a baseball field where relief pitchers can warm up; also used to refer to a team's relievers as a group.

debut
First appearance.

draft
A system that allows teams to acquire new players coming into a league.

general manager
An executive who runs a team and is responsible for finding and signing players.

no-hitter
A complete game in which a pitcher does not allow any hits.

perfect game
A complete game in which a pitcher retires every batter and allows no base runners.

professional
A person who gets paid to perform.

racism
Discriminating against other people based only on their race.

relief
An appearance by a pitcher who does not start the game.

rookie
A professional athlete in his or her first year of competition.

sacrifice fly
A fly ball out that advances, and often scores, a base runner.

veteran
A player who has played many years.

MORE INFORMATION

BOOKS

Flynn, Brendan. *The MLB Encyclopedia*. Minneapolis, MN: Abdo Publishing, 2022.

Gitlin, Marty. *MLB*. Minneapolis, MN: Abdo Publishing, 2021.

Hewson, Anthony K. *GOATs of Baseball*. Minneapolis, MN: Abdo Publishing, 2022.

ONLINE RESOURCES

To learn more about the Cincinnati Reds, please visit **abdobooklinks.com** or scan this QR code. These links are routinely monitored and updated to provide the most current information available.

INDEX

Anderson, Sparky, 26–27, 29, 33
Arroyo, Bronson, 39

Bates, Billy, 36
Bauer, Trevor, 40–41
Bench, Johnny, 25, 27, 30–31, 33
Billingham, Jack, 27
Browning, Tom, 34

Charlton, Norm, 35
Concepción, Dave, 26–27, 31
Crosley Jr., Powel, 14–16
Cueto, Johnny, 39

Davis, Eric, 34–36
Derringer, Paul, 17–20
Dibble, Rob, 35
Dunn, Adam, 38

Eller, Hod, 9–10

Foster, George, 27–28, 30

Gerónimo, César, 27
Greene, Hunter, 41
Griffey, Ken, 27, 29
Griffey Jr., Ken, 39
Groh, Heinie, 9
Gullett, Don, 27

Hatcher, Billy, 36

India, Jonathan, 41

Kluszewski, Ted, 20

Larkin, Barry, 34–37
Lombardi, Ernie, 16–17

McCormick, Frank, 19
Meyers, Billy, 19
Miley, Wade, 6
Morgan, Joe, 27, 29–30
Moustakas, Mike, 5–6
Myers, Randy, 35–36

Nolan, Gary, 27

Pérez, Tony, 25, 27, 29, 31, 33
Phillips, Brandon, 40
Piniella, Lou, 35

Rijo, José, 36
Ripple, Jimmy, 19
Robinson, Frank, 23, 25–26
Rose, Pete, 24–25, 27, 30–31, 33–35
Roush, Edd, 8, 11
Ruether, Dutch, 9

Sallee, Slim, 9

Vander Meer, Johnny, 16–17
Votto, Joey, 6, 39–41

Walters, Bucky, 17, 19–20

ABOUT THE AUTHOR

Anthony K. Hewson is a freelance writer originally from San Diego. He and his wife now live in the San Francisco Bay Area with their two dogs.